Janet Clarice Murray

Picture This

Indigo Dreams Publishing

First Edition: Picture This
First published in Great Britain in 2021 by:
Indigo Dreams Publishing Ltd
24 Forest Houses
Halwill
Beaworthy
EX21 5UU
www.indigodreams.co.uk

Janet Clarice Murray has asserted her right under the
Copyright, Designs and Patents Act 1988 to be identified as the
author of this work.
© 2021 Janet Clarice Murray

ISBN 978-1-912876-55-6

British Library Cataloguing in Publication Data. A CIP record
for this book can be obtained from the British Library.

Designed and typeset in Palatino Linotype by Indigo Dreams.
Cover design from artwork by Jane Burn
Printed and bound in Great Britain by 4edge Ltd.

Papers used by Indigo Dreams are recyclable products made
from wood grown in sustainable forests following the guidance
of the Forest Stewardship Council.

To Neil Reed and the Broomspring Writers

CONTENTS

Scene i 5

In Formation 6

My Garden 7

Brock 8

Rook 9

Cygnets at Beverley Brook 10

Pearls 11

Memoir in Purple 12

Masquerade 13

Imagining 14

Scene ii 15

Pasiphaë in the Park 16

Hollow Woman 17

Well-Dressing 18

Painted Aviary 19

Vernacular Green 20

Small Space 21

The Look of Love 22

Notes for a Poem about Love 23

How to Write a Conceptual Poem 24

Scene iii 25

Chinese Garden 26

Totems 27

The Colour Blue+ 28

Candlelight 29

Pochmurno 30

No Nightingales here 31

The Third Man 32

Dog days 33

Just a Spinning Leaf 34

Scene i

I stand at the end of the pier
looking out to the last point,
Dad's advice is
to do this when I'm sea-sick
but this is further and further where
stars dangle and the sea is black
no mackerel sky
scales glittering on the waves.
I can't even smile, I usually do,
when I picture the animals from the Tower
running through their tunnel
to paddle in the sea.
No seagull swooping on a beached razor shell.
I feel alone inside,
filled with dread that my parents will die
and I won't know where to find them.
I know this when I look
at the emptiness of sky
splashed by wild sea, its hugeness
when I compare it to me.

In Formation

Children squeeze paint
through doyleys stipple sky
with filigree cutting shapes
they unfold paper fan into figures
hand in hand birds flying
tail to beak horses trot
tail-flicks to flank.
        *
Pattern pulsates figures dancing
in line holding onto the waist
in front birds follow a leader
who tires then drops behind
replaced by another and horse-herds
gallop together, sometimes
one horse near the front
shows an eye bulging with fear.
        *
In Idlib small children scavenge
together scrabbling in a dump
for food for plastic. One finds
a pomegranate passes from hand
to hand torn apart. They chant
each lost-family-member but
only cry when they see other
children passing by in   formation
on their way to school.

My Garden

Beyond the chicken-wire fence
is an orchard lit by crab-apples,
patrolled by geese-guards.
My goose fear freezes grass while
sunlight sinks time so deep
it grows longer like saplings
in evening shade. I string a sweet-pea
frame, dig worms and feed the small ones
to hedgehogs, bolt when geese escape
honking and pecking at my feet.

I crawl through a hedge
to Archie's garden an old soldier
with one leg whose white eyes see
only shadows. My father slashes
a finger, scything long grass, it pours
blood, he paints it yellow
with iodine. I grow taller than red-hot
-pokers, festoon myself in nasturtium beads,
collect webs in curved privet-stems
still sparkling with dew.

My brother finds a Little-Owl builds
a wooden aviary, its wide eyes fade
to filmy grey, filtering out all grass
and trees in its long fateful gaze.

Brock

Whacked onto frosty grass,
his fur coat's soaked in melting ice
but his teeth don't chatter. His tribal stripe's there,
tapering arse curved to stumpy tail, muscly shoulders
bolted to giant feet, tipped with muddy claws.
I turn him with both hands, ruffle the fur along his spine,
part thin hair combed over belly-skin,
expose two pink studs, his baby nipples.
They prickle my DNA.

Rook

A papier-mâché bird held between both hands
no gloves. His chalky face shines on charcoal breast.
I prise fingers into wings, flaunt amethyst tints
fan tail wider, jink him into swoops and dives
tap his neck under stage-light, ruffle barred
neck feathers for flight. Straighten legs. He lands
stretches black toes on baize, pecks cardboard grass
picks up paper slugs. I pull back his sleek neck
open his bill, croak a story of courting a mate
feeding her worms and flies. I change hands, whirl
him round a calico sky to land on a tree-silhouette.
The bird topples, falls to the floor, snaps one leg.
He stops moving.
My hands appear.

Cygnets at Beverley Brook

They stalk from Barnes Pond
to breakfast at Beverley Brook on succulent
surface-weed, the occasional damsel-fly
glints green. Cob and pen look on
sometimes building a resting-nest
with splayed grass and bulrushes.

Fluff gives way to muscly chests,
waterproof feathers, first as shawls
then hat and scarf, dark grey
now white-flecked, sleeping in
window-display, heads under wings,
side by side on an apron of short grass.

They walk   they swim   as chests swell
after a hundred and twenty days
they'll launch   from a good run   necks prone
wings stretched   plumes pencilled   across
blue sky   they land   pulling wings back
skiing across water   then   splash-stop with
big-shaking-feathers   Now glossed
white from underneath   they'll gleam
a warning-light to other birds
from watery dais   Playfulness   whistling
on pen's back   forgotten   The cob
pecks them away   ready to build a new nest.

Pearls

When she first tries the crown, it's a snug fit,
her head the same size as her father's
— only she and the keeper allowed to touch.
She points to the ruby's hole where Henry V
stuck a feather, but the pearls, she senses
the pearls aren't happy, they need warm flesh
because they are alive.
She knows Elizabeth I's papyrus skin,
powdered with lead, was lit
by the lustre of pearls round her breast,
shone from the oyster mote, from lovers too
who allowed a pearl earring to tickle their lobe.
Maybe she sees a glint on membrane,
desire trapped in shell, hardened
to white-ball-baby tooth whose beauty shines
inward, more flesh than bone, dazzles
when threaded to hang round a throat, or pendulously
tremble on a crown,
which only she may stroke.

Memoir in Purple

She rolls a marble with clover inside
through lavender grass, which bends
glittering in storm light,
unpicks one small ray from a rainbow.
It crystallises
into Parma violet, not sweet enough
for taste buds which long
for Lovehearts, Cherry Lips, Allsorts.
She spits out mints, sucks
on a blackcurrant lolly
till her tongue turns mauve, trips
on a skipping rope, darkens her knee
like a ripening plum. On to the fair,
spins a dodgem, picks up
a broken lilac stem, then
splashes through waves, which dazzle her
with magenta light, roll her breathless
onto sand, wearing fish-tail
amethysts in her hair.

Masquerade

my black-haired Dad first-foots
the New Year picking coal from the shed
sooty wings sprout through his demob coat
I watch his face it splits

the phantom of a white-faced clown
peers through he blows on a coal-nut
conjures a diamond star hurls it
into Atlantic sky treads waves

stacks stones like an Inuk builds
inuksuit then dances around he loosens
his clothes galoshes stop his feet
getting wet he saves spare diamonds

for his harlequin suit lights a cigarette
with his wand we walk to a bar
his eyes turn to glass dazzle his friends
in reflected light chandeliers ring with his laugh

I run to the Ribble in wellies down
the estuary home a tune startles me
from the kitchen step he's playing
O Mein Papa on a golden trumpet

Imagining

starts with a line from the eye
still blurred between outside
and in, guided by smell
to the breast

where the world rests. Becomes
wavy line of ocean, serried antirrhinums
round the grass. Cirrus-clouds curling inside
puffed white when stomach's full,

biting wind when hungry.
By night ghosts seep through dreams
sucked back into a line
book-spine the edge of a tree

writing on wasps' nest
crumple of paper petticoat
catching words from long ago. Pressed
into pinned butterfly wings

suppressed under thunder clouds
painting a picture, a word which finds
a new space, sounds no longer
out of place, picking up the rhythm

of heart-beat, beak-tap on bark drum.
Wings flap, surprised by foot's tread
fill with dread inside a cat's mouth.
A pink-jam-wafer under a tongue, melts

like thick Antarctic snow, walks
on penguin feet, measures still life
by the length of a feather, a straw hat
background of pears and plums.

Scene ii

The corner of a picture curls
in my left thumb,
I can see the edge of a dream
the sleeve of a red robe pokes through
worn by what appears to be a woman
on a chaise-longue
playing a saxophone,
her left thumb presses the octave key.
I am outside looking in.
Is it me?

Pasiphaë in the Park

Lobelias peep through railings,
a red-robed woman is sprawling
on a chaise-longue. Dragged herself
from a lake with soggy chignon,
I've just fucked a white bull
she crows, her moon-face pocked
with bites. Corvids echo *caaaaw*,
but she's waltzing with peacocks freed
from their pen with falcons tearing
jackdaws. Scoops monarch butterflies
from milkweed, rips off their amber wings
to colour her eyes like a wolf.
She sits cross-legged, strokes her bull-baby
belly, scratches itchy toes in rosebeds.

Hollow Woman
(Leonora Carrington 1917-2011)

Leonora slips
out of shot-silk gown
into crimson feathers
with velvet cowl.

She inflates
over Bird Superior's green plumes
a monster bride with owl eyes
shrieking down.

One human eye
ink-blots her own menagerie
with lactating hyena, a rocking horse
bumps against the wall.

She flees to Mexico, paints red robes,
coifs horns — on a Minotaur
who delivers a daughter
spectral white.

Leonora's startled by her own face
at the window in debutante's veil
and feathered coronet.
She's tapping, whispers *let me in.*

Well-Dressing
(Bamford, Derbyshire)

St Mary's mouth bloats,
drawn on clay-board, outline
filled with hydrangea petals,
haricot beans stuff cheeks
set in a background of larch cones
circling the top of Fidler's Well.
Celebrates water's purity
roiling down Dark Peak
shaking moss and fronds.

St Mary replaces a Celtic god but
if her image is rubbed out
a river sprite could reappear
with Cupid's bow on fresh lips
beat damsel-wings down Winn Hill,
a quiver of arrows tied to her waist
to keep black-death away.

Painted Aviary

White-bellied green pigeon
red-headed bunting scarlet macaw
peacocks' eyes scorch dull feathers
beaks glint like razors the sky and meadows
are flight-beaten song-loud from when
the tiny raptors first chipped
out of the ice and soared in flocks
where wing never smudges wing.

Vernacular Green
(i.m. Howard Hodgkin 1932-2017)

Hodgkin sees common green
in privet, grass, chestnut husks
blown horsetail, chickweed
crushed under baby's toe
scum on ponds—pond weed.

Not silver olive, willow spinning
green or white, imported
rhododendron, clunking monkey
puzzle tree. Exempt montbretia's
erect leaves, circling

fiery tiger flowers, but if he glimpses
luminous green on the wing-tip
of an escaped parakeet, exposed
by pallid vernacular green, which
hides fairy wings sometimes,

in this moment he speaks
Indian green where a greener green
can be unleashed, somewhere between
emerald and jade, a brush dipped
in feathers round a teal duck's eye.

Small Space
(i.m. Stanley Spencer 1891-1959)

The small space
is ungetable
like next door's garden
where a thrush flies
over pear and walnut trees.

Small space to play
with the butcher's daughters
Fairy Dot steps
with bare tip-toes
on lily-pads not stones.

Small space fills
with ginger-haired girls
who look over railings
at a beehive
no bees inside.

Small attic space
calls from Macedonia
to finish a painting
the hubbub of swans
being marked.

On small canvas space
he captures the scene
white wings stretched wider
than church's angel wings
as sacred as

the holiest small space.
And when he returns
he walks the marguerite field
as it was when Sydney was alive
but the village cowls

have left
the small space
closed amid chimney smoke
no longer somewhere
somewhere else.

The Look of Love
(Hitchock's Notorious)

Montage of a woman hungover
notorious, uproarious, who cannot
love without the words.
Of a man who stares

teeters round her
she's a lighthouse
blinding him with a beam
no words can reflect.

Master-shot—
at the top of a stairwell
close-up her long-fingered hand
clutches the key to —

focus swirls to her crazed cup
it trembles in the wrong grasp.
A hall of mirror-faces drains
her countenance of light.

He wraps her in swagger-coat
carries her from the house
watches her face, nuzzles
I love you into the arc of her neck.

She opens her eyes, frowns,
slurs, *Why didn't you tell me
before?* His gaze drops to her toes,
painted like nacre shell.

Notes for a Poem about Love

A blue rooster in Trafalgar Square snorts
out colour through his bill
slicing mist more bravely than any sun.

Jasmine starbursts scattering
a November hedge, a lonely blackbird
singing at dusk, harbingers

more poignant than roses
in summer, swallows doing their thing. And —
St Anne's arm holding the Virgin Mary on her lap,

a friend who rubs the hollow between
shoulder blades, the scarf that Cary ties
round Ingrid's bare midriff,

a hand that plucks stray food from a chin,
the brush painting a swathe
of green round that brutal nude.

How to Write a Conceptual Poem

Don't just watch the bees
building in the crevices of your house —
see the house from inside the cracks
through bee-eyes. Cast thin chasms
with cold cure rubber, squeeze out the mould
like jelly-on-a-plate, fill with black bronze
bash the crumples, create a petrified meta-script.
Bend into a hopscotch, lay on a pavement
number the squares with chalk, throw
a small cinder — follow it— jump between edges
judder the mortar and erase it again.

Fold A4 paper then scalpel-cut
an Amazon journey along the crease, unfold
and cruise a picture-poem — melt a silver teaspoon
pull a metal skein, spin the tallest story so it crashes down
the full length of Niagara. Search the margins
of old books, find the stain of an ancient flood,
give it centre-stage and re-invent again.

Slash your forearm, forge the blood
into alphabet shapes. Read the letter A aloud
or a word containing A which can't sprout
from the ground without the pollen-dusting
that attracts the bees and, unlike the bees, resist
the scent of orange blossom wafting through the flues.

Scene iii

I catch Scarlatina, couldn't be meaner
at six years old. In isolation,
I sit at a bay window
eating cornflakes
so my parents won't worry as I look down
at two small people on the hospital lawn,
I suppose they are my parents. I am
only partly there I don't fully exist
without my tribe, see myself in their eyes,
hear their news listen to views see
the walls of my house distempered eau de nil.
And once I find chocolate under my pillow,
a nurse says my Dad has been
but because of Lady Scarlatina
he can't be let in. And
when I return home, my baby sister
is walking and my Mum looks
at me differently and nothing seems
the same so I know that everything
can change.

Chinese Garden
(a gift from China to Sydney, Australia)

Foo dogs guard the gate
into a miniature landscape, reflected
as a Tan Ying painting on the silky water
of Lake Brightness, rumpled
by koi fish who swim in summer water
bumping islands of pink lotus.
Lamp-light streams from a crag,
tries to melt rocks into leafy forest
while a smaller garden rises
through a moon-gate, revealed
with all the flourish
of a nesting doll, who pulls
out little copies of herself but is
unable to distract from the cinder-track
to the final resting place of old poets,
that black-stalked bamboo grove,
which struggles to hide night's terror
under a canopy of thick green leaves.

Totems
(Still Life with 'Hope', 1901)

When Gauguin went back to Tahiti,
he sent for sunflower seeds from Paris,
grew sunflowers in small clumps
to inspire his own still-lives,
flower-portraits of his dead friend
Van Gogh, a reminder of their time
together in the yellow house.
                    *

Studded in the background
of his sunflower picture is
a tiny painting of Hope by his friend
de Chavannes, a girl spread
on a white blanket, slim and vulnerable
blank featureless face.
                    *

He tucks in a print by Degas too,
hard to make out, colourless
in contrast to his foreground,
splashed by the colours
of a Meso-American pot,
the one holding the sunflowers
a Japanese bowl alongside.
                    *

In a corner of another painting
I thought I saw

                        a small goat-dog
                        red-pink.

The Colour Blue+
(i.m. my brother, Ian, d. 2017)

+darkens Skelly's pond
glazed by bugs and duck-weed
a narrow petrol skein sucks
purple from violets and ragged robin.

We caught tadpoles that shimmied
underneath. On the edge
gnarled old toes of trees tested
the water, kicked unwanted leaves.

+overcasts Cleveleys sands
there we trapped baby crabs which
freed on the kitchen lino
skittered like spiders.

I can still see water-spurts
by the ebbing sea which betrayed
cockles, signalling carelessly
where we should dig.

+re-shoots a Blackpool scene
when we strayed too far along a beach
the tide curved a treacherous arm
we waded up to our chins.

Later it would
drown the Chinese cocklers
in Morecambe Bay our harbinger
of lilies on your cask.

Their petals flutter like butterflies
red admiral and tortoiseshell
maybe they'll lift blue shadow
from my face dazzle me with red.

Candlelight

Curves of the flame shift,
drawing the edge of dark, shrink
then inflate the space, suck me in
like a moth, shape a place in my mind
for thought, as the flame beams inwards
to that dark seam always there,
under the bed. And a hollow-eyed ghost
blows through a hollow mouth
snuffs the candle out, takes back
the halo of space, reduces the room in my head
to a small white hole.

Pochmurno

The word is poch-mur-no,
it clouds my mind,
cloudy in Polish,
rounds my palate,
the rusty resonance of
guttural sound
like lumpy clouds
hanging over Cottonopolis
soaked by raindrops
from Victorian sky, defaults
mizzle,
trickles drizzle
teems stair-rods bouncing
off ground so damp
the cotton threads can't snap.
My nearest word
is pockmark when rain
taps holes in snow
and at night pocks
crust in frost glitter
with stardust enough
to fill an egg-cup next day.

No Nightingales here
(Lublin, Poland)

Look down at your feet in Saski Park
follow bone-stemmed crow feathers
pursue a revenant who mixes them with mud
smears elbow gloves fledges

black wings over John Paul's head
casts dark shadow on his watered silk
wraps it round the Opera House
lands on the bus to Majdanek

shits lime in Colonel Sanders' eye
as it searches for Gestapo HQ
pecks at a marigold petal path
to Marshall Piłsudski on horse-back

fountains splash cobalt blue
acrobats teeter on Baroque sills —stop
stand still — it roosts on Grodzka Gate
shakes loose feathers on the other side

folds wings into hunch back
cracks a dead bluebottle
no birdsong.

The Third Man
(Director's notes)

A cat nibbles Harry Lime's shoes,
the lit window reveals him
in a doorway, alive not dead
as supposed. Shot by friend Holly,
in the sewers, torch lights swirl round
tunnels like rapiers. This time,
Harry's supposed to die. Of course
the actor will get up in a minute.
I can buy glycerine, put drops
in Anna's eyes and she'll cry for Harry.
Sometimes I manage to film real tears.
Now I've got glycerine, I'm frightened
of the real thing. Deep angled shots,
vibrato zither, no colour, as Anna links arms
with Holly and walks a lifetime down
Zentralfriedhof Avenue. That ending's
on the cutting room floor. She walks
past him without so much as a second glance.

Dog days

Here come the dog days
wagging their tails,
a full-blown balloon wrenched
from my hand is zig-zagging
over ears of corn and
wide-open faces of sunflowers.
I hear my own scream as a missile
shoots down a super moon.
It's come too close to the earth.
Children run
with hair on fire
and I can't see Autumn over the brow
only moonlight mistaken for dawn.
It's like the landing of the asteroid
that polished off
tyrannosaurs, and ichthyosaurs
scattered their scales, feathers
and toe nails into the crust of the earth.
Is this how it feels before a war?
We're drinking tea
from china cups,
a sunbeam shines through a window,
and a shadow falls
on a Schubert nocturne
played by a man
with starched collar and bow tie.

Just a Spinning Leaf

Raining, through the window
I glimpse a small leaf, spinning
endlessly. I step outside, into

a strand of web—the leaf flutters
web loops my mouth. I spit it out,
the leaf lands on the floor, an illusion

of infinity through my French window
sculpted by a spider in the rain.

Acknowledgements

The author would like to acknowledge the following people and groups: Maurice Riordan, Faber Poet and her tutor as Professor of Poetry at Sheffield Hallam University, Poetry Room (Sheffield), Leadbelly Poets & The Poetry School, Barnes and Chiswick Stanzas.

Picture This is Janet Clarice Murray's debut collection.

Indigo Dreams Publishing Ltd
24, Forest Houses
Cookworthy Moor
Halwill
Beaworthy
Devon
EX21 5UU
www.indigodreams.co.uk